D1355816

GREAT EGG
COOKBOOK

Consultant Editor:
Valerie Ferguson

LORENZ BOOKS

Introduction

Eggs are surely the most amazing natural food available to us. Not only are they rich in nutrients, including protein, vitamins A and B and iron, but they are also outstandingly versatile. They can be soft-boiled, hard-boiled, poached, coddled, baked, fried or scrambled; made into omelettes, soufflés, custards, batters and meringues, and added to sauces, soups, pastry and cakes.

Although fresh eggs taste wonderful in their own right, they can be combined successfully with all kinds of other flavours, savoury or sweet. From the simple but elegant Omelette with Herbs to more elaborate special-occasion dishes such as Celeriac & Blue Cheese Roulade, this book provides tasters of the many ways to prepare eggs. Try the pretty Egg Flower Soup, the aromatic Lentils with Baked Eggs, or the intriguingly named dessert Floating Islands. Enjoy classic scrambled eggs with a twist in Toasted Brioche with Scrambled Eggs & Morels, or sample delicious Quail's Egg & Vermouth Tartlets for a celebration treat.

There are enough ways of preparing eggs to provide many pleasurable hours of cooking and eating, so get cracking now!

All About Eggs

If you follow the simple advice below you will get the best results.

Types of Eggs

Hens' eggs are the type most widely produced and eaten in this country. There is no difference between brown or white shells – the colour simply denotes the breed of hen. Duck and goose eggs are also sometimes available from farms or delicatessens. Duck eggs are useful for cakes and puddings – one ducks' egg, for example, can be substituted for 1½–2 hens' eggs. Quails' eggs, which are small and have attractively marked shells, used to be regarded as a luxury, but are now sold in larger supermarkets; they are ideal for special occasion dishes.

The vast majority of hens' eggs are produced by birds housed in intensive battery units: that is, in huge groups of small cages with several birds to a cage. You will also find on supermarket shelves non-battery eggs labelled "barn","free-range" and "organic". Barn eggs are laid by hens housed indoors but with the ability to move about freely, though conditions are still crowded. Free-range eggs are from birds with access during daylight hours to outdoor runs containing vegetation. Organic eggs are produced by hens housed similarly to free-range birds, but on land untreated with chemicals.

Above: Duck eggs are larger and more elongated than hens' eggs.

Above, clockwise from top left: Bantam, brown hens', pullets', quails' and white hens' eggs can all be used in cooking.

Storage and Hygiene

To keep eggs as fresh as possible, it is advisable to store them in the fridge. Remember to remove them at least 30 minutes before cooking, to come to room temperature. A cool larder is an acceptable alternative if you use eggs frequently; buy small quantities in any case to ensure that they are fresh.

Wherever you store eggs, keep them in the boxes supplied and well away from any strong-smelling foods, because they can easily absorb flavours through their porous shells.

Although the problem of salmonella has been dealt with by precautions during egg production, we still need to follow basic hygiene rules when cooking with eggs. Wash the shells well before use and wash your hands and utensils as soon as possible after preparing raw eggs. Anyone who could be particularly vulnerable to bacterial infection, such as very young children, pregnant women and elderly people, should not eat raw or lightly cooked eggs.

Freshness

Different recipes require eggs of varying ages, although all eggs are best used within 2 weeks. For simple soft-boiling, frying and poaching, the freshest eggs taste the best, and they make the nicest cakes; they are also the easiest to separate (though eggs up to 1 week old are still fine for this). Do not attempt to use very fresh eggs for hard-boiling as they will not peel successfully. For scrambling, omelettes, custards, quiches and other baked dishes, eggs up to 2 weeks old will perform well.

Techniques

Boiling Eggs

Soft-boiling Eggs

1 Bring a pan of water to the boil. Using a slotted spoon, lower in each egg.

2 Reduce the heat and simmer for 3–5 minutes depending on how firm you like the egg white (the yolk will be runny).

Hard-boiling Eggs

Cook as for soft-boiled eggs, but for 10 minutes. Then immediately plunge the eggs into iced water: this helps prevent a grey layer from forming round the yolk. When cool enough to handle, peel away the shells.

Poaching Eggs

1 Bring a large pan of water to the boil. Break each egg and slip it gently into the water. Reduce the heat and simmer for 3–4 minutes or until the eggs are cooked.

2 With a slotted spoon, lift out each egg and drain on kitchen paper. Trim the egg white to a neat shape with a knife or kitchen scissors.

THE SETTING FACTOR: If your eggs are not really fresh, adding white wine vinegar to the poaching water will help the egg white to coagulate, although it will slightly flavour the egg.

Frying Eggs

1 Heat butter, bacon fat or oil (to cover the bottom generously) in a frying pan until sizzling. Break each egg and slip it into the pan.

Scrambling Eggs

Tender, creamy scrambled eggs are perfect for breakfast or brunch, but you can also add flavourings for a more unusual snack or supper dish.

2 Fry for 1–1½ minutes or until the egg white is just set and opaque or more firm, according to your taste. Carefully lift the egg from the pan using a fish slice.

1 In a small bowl, beat the eggs with a little salt and pepper, using a fork, until they are well blended. Melt a generous knob of butter in a frying pan over a low heat and pour in the beaten eggs.

Separating Eggs

Tap the egg against the edge of a bowl to break the shell across the middle, taking care not to break the yolk. Pull the two halves of shell apart and gently tip the yolk from one to the other, letting the white run into the bowl.

2 Cook, scraping up and turning the eggs over, for 3–5 minutes or until they are softly set and still moist. Take care not to overcook the eggs, which will continue to cook in the hot pan even after it has been removed from the heat.

Toasted Brioche with Scrambled Eggs & Morels

The richness of scrambled eggs marries wonderfully with cream, Madeira and the full-bodied flavour of morels.

Serves 4

INGREDIENTS
150 g/5 oz/2 cups fresh or 15 g/½ oz/
   ¼ cup dried morels
25 g/1 oz/2 tbsp unsalted butter
1 shallot, finely chopped
60 ml/4 tbsp Madeira
60 ml/4 tbsp crème fraîche
4 small brioches
salt and freshly ground
   black pepper

FOR THE SCRAMBLED EGGS
8 eggs
60 ml/4 tbsp crème fraîche
25 g/1 oz/2 tbsp
   unsalted butter

1 If using dried morels, cover with warm water, soak for 20 minutes and drain. Melt the butter in a non-stick frying pan and gently fry the shallot until it is softened.

2 Add the drained or fresh morels to the frying pan and cook briefly, then stir in the Madeira and continue to cook until the liquid is syrupy.

3 Stir in the crème fraîche and simmer briefly. Season, transfer to a bowl and keep warm.

4 Remove the tops from the brioches and toast both halves under a moderate grill until lightly browned.

5 To make the scrambled eggs, beat together the eggs, crème fraîche and seasoning using a fork. Melt the butter in the frying pan, pour in the egg mixture and cook, stirring continuously, until slightly cooked. Remove from the heat.

6 Spoon the scrambled eggs (which will have continued cooking in their own heat) over the lower halves of the brioches, followed by the morels. Rest the upper brioche halves on top and serve.

VARIATION: Madeira provides an oaky, hazelnut flavour to balance stronger-tasting mushrooms. You can also use a medium-dry sherry.

11

Champagne Truffle Breakfast

Smooth scrambled eggs with truffle, served with champagne, make the perfect celebration breakfast. For the best flavour, it is worth tracking down a fresh truffle.

Serves 4

INGREDIENTS
4 brioches
8 free-range eggs
60 ml/4 tbsp crème fraîche
3 drops truffle oil (optional)
1 fresh black truffle
25 g/1 oz/2 tbsp unsalted butter,
    plus extra for spreading
salt and freshly ground
    black pepper
champagne or Buck's fizz,
    to serve

1 Preheat a moderate grill. Cut the brioches in two horizontally, toast and keep warm.

2 Break the eggs into a jug, add the crème fraîche and truffle oil, if using. Do not add more than a few drops of oil or the flavour will be bitter. Season and beat with a fork. Finely slice half the truffle into the egg mixture.

3 Just before you are ready to serve, melt the butter in a frying pan and pour in the eggs. With a flat wooden spoon, stir the base of the pan until the eggs are lightly scrambled. They should be a little underdone.

4 Butter both halves of each toasted brioche and arrange on four warmed serving plates.

5 Spoon the scrambled egg on to each brioche half and scatter with shavings from the remaining truffle half. Serve with champagne or Buck's fizz (champagne and orange juice).

Huevos Rancheros

Conjure up the Wild West with this Tex-Mex dish in which fried eggs are served with refried beans on tortillas.

Serves 4

INGREDIENTS
480 g/17 oz can refried beans
300 ml/½ pint/1¼ cups
    enchilada sauce
oil, for frying
4 corn tortillas
4 eggs
150 g/5 oz/1¼ cups grated Monterey
    Jack or Cheddar cheese
salt and freshly ground
    black pepper

1 Heat the refried beans and the enchilada sauce in separate saucepans. Cover both pans and set them aside until needed. Preheat the oven to 110°C/225°F/Gas ¼.

2 Pour a 5 mm/¼ in depth of the oil into a small, non-stick frying pan and heat. Add the tortillas, one at a time, to the hot oil, and fry them for about 30 seconds on each side until they are just crisp.

3 Drain the tortillas on kitchen paper, and keep them warm on a baking sheet in the oven. Discard the oil used for frying.

4 Let the frying pan cool slightly, then wipe it with kitchen paper to remove all but a film of oil and fry two of the eggs until the whites are just set. Season with salt and freshly ground pepper, then transfer to the oven to keep warm. Cook the remaining eggs in the same way.

5 To serve, place a tortilla on each of four plates. Spread a layer of refried beans over each tortilla, then top with an egg. Spoon over the warm enchilada sauce, sprinkle with the cheese and serve.

VARIATION: If you are really pushed for time, this dish may be served on a layer of unflavoured tortilla chips instead.

Eggs Benedict

A classic and elegant dish that combines poached eggs with ham and creamy hollandaise sauce.

Serves 4

INGREDIENTS
5 ml/1 tsp vinegar
4 eggs
2 English muffins or 4 slices bread
butter, for spreading
2 slices cooked ham, 5 mm/¼ in thick,
  cut in half crossways
fresh chives, to garnish
salad, to serve

FOR THE SAUCE
3 egg yolks
30 ml/2 tbsp lemon juice
1.5 ml/¼ tsp salt
225 g/8 oz/1 cup butter
30 ml/2 tbsp single cream
freshly ground black pepper

1 To make the hollandaise sauce, put the egg yolks with the lemon juice and salt in a food processor and process for 15 seconds to combine. Melt the butter in a small saucepan until it bubbles (do not let it brown).

2 With the motor running, pour the hot butter into the processor through the feed tube in a slow, steady stream. Turn off the machine as soon as all the butter has been added.

3 Scrape the sauce into the top of a double boiler, over just-simmering water. Stir the mixture for 2–3 minutes until it has thickened. (If the sauce curdles, whisk in 15 ml/1 tbsp boiling water.)

4 Stir the cream into the sauce and season to taste with freshly ground black pepper. Keep warm over the hot water.

5 Bring a pan of water to the boil. Stir in the vinegar. Break each egg into a cup, then slide it carefully into the water.

6 Cook each egg for 3–4 minutes until set to your taste. Drain on kitchen paper. Carefully trim any ragged edges off the eggs.

7 Meanwhile, split and toast the muffins or toast the bread slices. Butter while still warm.

8 Place a piece of ham on each muffin half or slice of toast. Place a poached egg on top and spoon over the warm hollandaise sauce. Garnish with fresh chives and serve with salad.

Egg & Cheese Soup

As the egg cooks it gives this rich soup a creamy texture.

Serves 6

INGREDIENTS
3 eggs
45 ml/3 tbsp fine semolina
90 ml/6 tbsp freshly grated
    Parmesan cheese
pinch of nutmeg
1.5 litres/2½ pints/6¼ cups meat or
    chicken stock, cooled
salt and freshly ground
    black pepper
12 slices French bread, to serve

1 Beat the eggs in a bowl with the semolina, cheese, nutmeg and 250 ml/ 8 fl oz/1 cup of the cool stock.

2 Meanwhile, pour the remaining stock into a large saucepan and heat it until it reaches simmering point.

3 A few minutes before you are ready to serve the soup, whisk the egg mixture into the stock. Raise the heat slightly and bring it barely to the boil. Season with salt and freshly ground black pepper. Cook for 3–4 minutes. As the egg cooks, the soup will not be completely smooth.

4 Toast the bread and place two slices in the bottom of each soup plate. Ladle the hot soup over the bread and serve the dish immediately.

Egg Flower Soup

The egg sets into pretty strands, giving the soup a flowery look.

Serves 6

INGREDIENTS
1 litre/1¾ pints/4 cups stock
45 ml/3 tbsp light soy sauce
30 ml/2 tbsp dry sherry
    or vermouth
3 spring onions, diagonally sliced
small piece of fresh root ginger,
    peeled and shredded
4 large lettuce leaves, shredded
5 ml/1 tsp sesame oil
2 eggs, beaten
salt and freshly ground
    black pepper
sesame seeds, to garnish

1 Pour the stock into a large saucepan. Add all the ingredients except the eggs and sesame seeds. Bring the mixture to the boil and cook for about 2 minutes.

2 Very carefully, pour the eggs in a thin, steady stream into the centre of the boiling liquid.

3 Count to three, then quickly stir the soup. The egg will begin to cook and form long threads. Season to taste, ladle the soup into warm bowls and serve immediately, sprinkled with sesame seeds.

Hard-boiled Eggs with Tuna Sauce

The combination of eggs with a tasty tuna mayonnaise makes a nourishing first course that is quick and easy to prepare.

Serves 6

INGREDIENTS

6 extra-large eggs
200 g/7 oz can tuna in olive oil
3 canned anchovy fillets
15 ml/1 tbsp capers, drained
30 ml/2 tbsp lemon juice
60 ml/4 tbsp olive oil
freshly ground black pepper
salt (optional)
extra capers and anchovy fillets,
    to garnish (optional)

FOR THE MAYONNAISE

1 egg yolk, at room temperature
5 ml/1 tsp Dijon mustard
5 ml/1 tsp white wine vinegar or
    lemon juice
150 ml/¼ pint/⅔ cup olive oil

1 Start by hard-boiling the eggs for 12–14 minutes. Drain and immediately plunge into a bowl of cold water. Peel carefully and set aside.

VARIATIONS: Cider vinegar can be used instead of white wine vinegar for the mayonnaise, if necessary. You can also use vegetable oil instead of olive oil, although the flavour is not so good.

2 To make the mayonnaise, whisk the egg yolk, mustard and vinegar or lemon juice together in a small bowl. Whisk in the oil a few drops at a time until 45–60 ml/3–4 tbsp has been incorporated. Pour in the remainder in a slow stream, whisking constantly.

3 Place the tuna with its oil, the anchovies, capers, lemon juice and olive oil in a blender or a food processor. Process until smooth.

4 Fold the tuna sauce into the mayonnaise. Season with pepper and salt if needed. Chill for at least 1 hour.

5 To serve, cut the cooled hard-boiled eggs in half lengthways. Arrange in an attractive pattern on a serving platter. Spoon the chilled tuna sauce over the eggs and garnish with the extra drained capers and anchovy fillets, if desired. Serve chilled.

Parmesan & Poached Egg Salad with Croûtons

Soft poached eggs, hot garlic croûtons and cool, crisp salad leaves make an unforgettable combination.

Serves 2

INGREDIENTS
½ small loaf white bread
75 ml/5 tbsp extra virgin olive oil
2 eggs, broken into separate bowls
115 g/4 oz mixed salad leaves
2 garlic cloves, crushed
7.5 ml/1½ tsp white wine vinegar
25 g/1 oz Parmesan cheese shavings
freshly ground black pepper

1 Remove the crust from the bread. Cut the bread into 2.5 cm/1 in cubes. Heat 30 ml/2 tbsp of the oil in a frying pan. Cook the bread cubes for about 5 minutes, tossing occasionally, until they are golden brown.

2 Meanwhile, bring a pan of water to the boil. Carefully slide in the eggs, one at a time. Gently poach the eggs in the water for 3–4 minutes until they are lightly cooked.

3 Place the mixed salad leaves on two serving plates. Remove the croûtons from the frying pan and then arrange them over the leaves. Wipe the pan clean with kitchen paper.

4 Heat the remaining oil in the pan, add the garlic and vinegar and cook over high heat for 1 minute. Pour the warm dressing over each salad.

5 Place a poached egg on each portion of salad. Scatter with shavings of Parmesan cheese and a little freshly ground black pepper.

COOK'S TIP: Adding a dash of vinegar to the water, before poaching the eggs, helps to keep the whites together. To ensure that a poached egg has a good shape, swirl the water with a spoon, whirlpool-fashion, before sliding in the egg.

Baked Eggs with Tarragon

Traditional cocotte dishes or small ramekins can be used for this recipe, as either will take one egg perfectly.

Serves 4

INGREDIENTS
40 g/1½ oz/3 tbsp butter, softened, for
    greasing and baking
120 ml/4 fl oz/½ cup double cream
15–30 ml/1–2 tbsp chopped
    fresh tarragon
4 eggs
salt and freshly ground
    black pepper
fresh tarragon sprigs,
    to garnish

2 Meanwhile, gently warm the double cream in a small saucepan. Sprinkle some chopped fresh tarragon into the bottom of each ovenproof dish, then spoon a little of the warmed cream over the layer of tarragon.

1 Preheat the oven to 180°C/350°F/ Gas 4. Lightly butter four small ovenproof dishes, then warm them in the oven for a few minutes.

VARIATION: You might like to try baking eggs with other herbs: chervil, marjoram and rosemary also work well.

3 Carefully break an egg on top of the cream in each of the prepared ovenproof dishes, season each egg with salt and freshly ground black pepper according to taste, and then spoon a little more of the warmed double cream over each of the eggs. Sprinkle over a little more chopped tarragon.

4 Add a knob of butter to each dish and place them in a roasting tin containing sufficient water to come halfway up the sides of the dishes. Bake for 8–10 minutes until the whites are just set and the yolks still soft. Serve hot, garnished with tarragon sprigs.

Quail's Egg & Vermouth Tartlets

Eggs hard-boiled in this way have an attractive marbled surface which gives them an intriguing appearance.

Serves 4

INGREDIENTS
10 quail's eggs
30 ml/2 tbsp soy sauce
30 ml/2 tbsp mustard seeds
15 ml/1 tbsp green tea leaves
6 filo pastry sheets, thawed if frozen
50 g/2 oz/¼ cup butter, melted
1 small avocado, peeled
    and stoned
45 ml/3 tbsp dry white vermouth
30 ml/2 tbsp mayonnaise
10 ml/2 tsp lime juice
salt and freshly ground
    black pepper
paprika, for dusting
lamb's lettuce, to serve

1 Put the quail's eggs into a saucepan. Pour over enough cold water to cover. Add the soy sauce, mustard seeds and green tea leaves. Bring the water to the boil, then lower the heat and allow to simmer for 3 minutes.

VARIATION: Pack cooked, shelled eggs into wide-necked sterilized jars and cover with dry sherry or vermouth. Seal, label and store in a cool place. Use within 6 weeks.

2 Remove the pan from the heat and lift out the quail's eggs with a slotted spoon. Gently tap them on a firm surface so that the shells crack all over. Put the eggs back into the liquid in the pan and leave in a cool place for 8 hours or overnight.

3 Preheat the oven to 190°C/375°F/ Gas 5. Grease four 10 cm/4 in tartlet tins. Brush each sheet of filo pastry with a little melted butter and stack the six sheets on top of each other. Stamp out four rounds of pastry with a 15 cm/6 in cutter.

4 Line the tins with the layers of pastry and frill the edges. Put a crumpled piece of foil in each filo case and bake in the oven for 12–15 minutes until cooked and golden. Remove the piece of foil from each filo case and leave to cool.

5 In a food processor, process the avocado, vermouth, mayonnaise, lime juice and seasoning until smooth.

6 Shell and halve the eggs. Pipe or spoon the avocado mixture into the pastry cases and arrange the halved eggs on top. Dust with paprika and serve with lamb's lettuce.

Omelette with Herbs

Fresh herbs and crème fraîche make a delicious omelette filling.

Serves 1

INGREDIENTS
2 eggs
15 g/½ oz/1 tbsp butter
15 ml/1 tbsp crème fraîche or
    soured cream
5 ml/1 tsp chopped fresh mixed herbs
    (such as tarragon, chives, parsley
    or marjoram)
salt and freshly ground
    black pepper

1 Beat together the eggs and seasoning. Melt the butter in an omelette pan or small, non-stick frying pan until it is foaming, then pour in the eggs.

2 As the egg mixture starts to set, lift up the sides using a palette knife and tilt the pan to allow the uncooked egg to run underneath. When the egg is just set, spoon the crème fraîche or soured cream down the centre and sprinkle with the herbs.

3 To serve the omelette, hold the pan over a warmed plate. With a palette knife, lift one edge of the omelette and fold it over the middle. Tilt the pan to help the omelette fold over on itself in thirds, then slide it out on to the plate.

Egg-stuffed Tomatoes

A simple but colourful egg dish, served with herby mayonnaise.

Serves 4

INGREDIENTS
175 ml/6 fl oz/¾ cup mayonnaise
30 ml/2 tbsp chopped
    fresh chives
30 ml/2 tbsp chopped fresh basil
30 ml/2 tbsp chopped
    fresh parsley
4 hard-boiled eggs, peeled
4 ripe medium tomatoes
salt
lettuce, to serve

1 In a small bowl, blend together the mayonnaise and herbs and set aside. Using an egg slicer or sharp knife, cut the eggs into thin slices.

2 Place the tomatoes core-end down and make deep cuts to within 1 cm/½ in of the base. (There should be the same number of cuts in each tomato as there are slices of egg; the white ends of the eggs can be discarded.)

3 Fan open the tomatoes and sprinkle with salt, then insert an egg slice into each slit. Serve with lettuce and the herb mayonnaise.

Right: Omelette with Herbs (top);
Egg-stuffed Tomatoes

Pepper & Potato Tortilla

A tortilla, which is rather like a thick omelette or pastryless quiche, is best eaten cold, cut into chunky wedges.

Serves 4

INGREDIENTS
2 medium potatoes
about 45 ml/3 tbsp olive oil
1 large onion, thinly sliced
2 garlic cloves, crushed
1 green pepper, seeded and
   thinly sliced
1 red pepper, seeded and thinly sliced
6 eggs, beaten
115 g/4 oz/1 cup mature cheese, grated
salt and freshly ground
   black pepper
finely chopped fresh parsley, to garnish

1 Do not peel the potatoes, but wash them thoroughly. Par-boil them in salted water for about 10 minutes, then drain and thickly slice.

2 In a large, non-stick frying pan, heat the oil and fry the onion, garlic and the green and red pepper slices for about 5 minutes until they have softened. Meanwhile, preheat the grill.

3 Add the potato slices to the pan and continue frying, stirring occasionally, until the potatoes are completely cooked and the other vegetables are soft. Add a little extra oil if the pan seems rather dry.

4 Pour in half the eggs, then sprinkle over half the cheese followed by the rest of the eggs, seasoning as you go. Finish with a layer of cheese. Continue to cook over a low heat, without stirring, half-covering the pan with a lid to help set the eggs.

5 When the mixture is firm, flash the pan under the hot grill to seal the top lightly. Leave the tortilla in the pan to cool. This helps it firm up and makes it easier to turn out. Garnish with parsley.

VARIATION: You can add any sliced and lightly cooked vegetable, such as mushrooms, courgettes or broccoli, instead of peppers.

Vegetable Stir-fry with Eggs

In this dish, eggs are lightly cooked nestling in a bed of courgettes, peppers, onions and tomatoes and topped with melted cheese.

Serves 4

INGREDIENTS
30 ml/2 tbsp olive oil
1 onion, roughly chopped
2 garlic cloves, crushed
175 g/6 oz cooked ham
225 g/8 oz courgettes
1 red pepper, seeded and
 thinly sliced
1 yellow pepper, seeded and
 thinly sliced
10 ml/2 tsp paprika
400 g/14 oz can chopped tomatoes
15 ml/1 tbsp sun-dried tomato purée
4 eggs
115 g/4 oz/1 cup Cheddar
 cheese, grated
salt and freshly ground black pepper

1 Heat the oil in a deep frying pan and cook the onion and garlic for 4 minutes or until beginning to soften. Meanwhile, cut the ham and courgettes into 5 cm/2 in long strips. Set the ham aside.

2 Add the courgettes and peppers to the onion and cook over a medium heat for 3–4 minutes or until beginning to soften.

3 Stir in the paprika, chopped tomatoes, sun-dried tomato purée, strips of ham and seasoning. Bring the mixture to the boil and allow to simmer gently for 15 minutes, or until the vegetables are just tender.

4 Reduce the heat to a low setting. Make four wells in the vegetable mixture, then carefully break an egg into each one and add seasoning. Cook over a gentle heat until the egg white is beginning to set.

5 Preheat the grill to hot. Protect the frying pan handle with foil. Sprinkle the grated cheese over the eggs and place under the hot grill to cook for about 5 minutes until the cheese is melted and golden and the eggs are lightly set. Serve at once.

Eggs Flamenco

In this recipe, eggs are oven-baked in individual dishes of colourful mixed Mediterranean vegetables.

Serves 4

INGREDIENTS
2 red peppers
1 green pepper
30 ml/2 tbsp olive oil
1 large onion, finely sliced
2 garlic cloves, crushed
5–6 tomatoes, peeled and chopped
120 ml/4 fl oz/½ cup puréed canned
    tomatoes or tomato juice
good pinch of dried basil
4 eggs
45 ml/3 tbsp single cream
pinch of cayenne
    pepper (optional)
salt and freshly ground
    black pepper
French or Spanish bread, to serve

2 Add the peppers to the pan and fry for 10 minutes. Stir in the tomatoes and purée or juice, the basil and seasoning. Cook gently for a further 10 minutes until the peppers are soft.

3 Spoon the mixture into four ovenproof dishes. Make a hollow in the centre and break an egg into each. Spoon 10 ml/2 tsp cream over the yolk of each egg and sprinkle with a little black pepper or cayenne, as preferred.

1 Preheat the oven to 180°C/350°F/ Gas 4. Seed and thinly slice the peppers. Heat the oil in a large frying pan and fry the onion and garlic gently for about 5 minutes, stirring, until softened.

4 Bake for 12–15 minutes until the white of the egg is lightly set. Serve at once with chunks of warm, crusty French or Spanish bread.

Tuna Frittata

This open omelette, densely packed with delicious vegetables and fish, is the ultimate one-pan meal.

Serves 2–3

INGREDIENTS
25 g/1 oz/2 tbsp butter
15 ml/1 tbsp olive oil
1 onion, finely chopped
175 g/6 oz courgettes, halved lengthways
  and sliced
75 g/3 oz/scant 1¼ cups brown-cap
  mushrooms, sliced
50 g/2 oz asparagus tips
4 eggs
75 g/3 oz/6 tbsp soft cheese
30 ml/2 tbsp chopped fresh thyme
200 g/7 oz can tuna in brine, drained and
  roughly flaked
115 g/4 oz cooked peeled prawns
salt and freshly ground black pepper

2 In a bowl, beat together the eggs, soft cheese, thyme and plenty of seasoning until well combined.

3 Stir the flaked tuna into the pan. Add the prawns and season well with salt and freshly ground black pepper. Heat through gently. Pour in the egg mixture and cook over a gentle heat for about 5 minutes until the egg begins to set.

COOK'S TIP: For best results, try not to break up the flakes of tuna too much when stirring them into the pan.

1 Heat the butter and oil in a medium-size, preferably non-stick frying pan. Cook the onion for 3 minutes. Add the courgettes, mushrooms and asparagus and cook for a further 10 minutes or until beginning to soften and brown.

4 As the egg sets, push it away from the sides to allow uncooked egg to run on to the base of the pan. Preheat the grill to medium. Protect the handle of the frying pan with foil and place under the grill to set and brown the surface of the frittata. Serve immediately, cut into wedges.

Irish Colcannon

A lovely, warming winter's dish in which baked eggs nestle among
creamy potatoes with curly kale or green cabbage, and are topped with
a sprinkling of grated cheese.

Serves 4

INGREDIENTS

1 kg/2¼ lb potatoes, cut into
    even pieces
225 g/8 oz/2½ cups curly kale or crisp
    green cabbage, rinsed, stems removed
    and leaves shredded
2 spring onions, chopped
butter or margarine,
    to taste
freshly grated nutmeg
4 large eggs
75 g/3 oz/¾ cup mature
    cheese, freshly grated (such as Cheddar,
    Red Leicester or Lancashire)
salt and freshly ground
    black pepper

3 Drain the kale or green cabbage
and mix into the mashed potato with
the onions, butter or margarine and
nutmeg. Season to taste with salt and
freshly ground black pepper.

1 Cook the potatoes in a large
saucepan of lightly salted boiling
water until they are just tender. Drain
the potatoes well and mash them
thoroughly with a potato masher or
through a fine Mouli.

2 Lightly cook the shredded kale or
green cabbage until it is just tender
but still retains its crispness. Preheat
the oven to 190°C/375°F/Gas 5.

4 Spoon the mixture into a shallow,
ovenproof dish. Make four hollows in
the mixture, crack an egg into each
one and season well.

COOK'S TIP: Choose an attractive
ovenproof dish which you can bring
to the table.

5 Place in the oven to bake for about 12 minutes or until the eggs are just set, but the yolks are not hard, then sprinkle evenly with the grated cheese and serve immediately.

VARIATIONS: A whole range of other vegetables can be used as a "bed" for baking eggs. French beans, Brussels sprouts and spinach are just a few you might like to try.

Lentils with Baked Eggs

An unusual combination of red lentils, herbs and eggs.

Serves 4

INGREDIENTS
450 g/1 lb/2 cups red lentils
3 leeks, thinly sliced
10 ml/2 tsp coriander seeds,
  finely crushed
15 ml/1 tbsp chopped fresh coriander
30 ml/2 tbsp chopped fresh mint
15 ml/1 tbsp red wine vinegar
1 litre/1¾ pints/4 cups
  vegetable stock
4 eggs
salt and freshly ground black pepper
chopped fresh parsley,
  to garnish

1 Put the lentils in a deep saucepan. Add the leeks, coriander seeds, fresh coriander, mint, vinegar and stock.

2 Bring to the boil, then lower the heat and simmer for 30–40 minutes or until the lentils are cooked and have absorbed all the liquid.

3 Preheat the oven to 180°C/350°F/ Gas 4. Season the lentil mixture generously with salt and freshly ground black pepper and divide among four lightly greased baking dishes.

4 Using the back of a spoon, make a hollow in the lentil mixture in each dish. Break an egg into each hollow.

5 Cover each of the dishes with a layer of foil and bake in the oven for 15–20 minutes or until the eggs are set. Sprinkle with plenty of chopped fresh parsley and serve at once.

Persian Spinach Omelette

Nuts, herbs and vegetables flavour this egg dish.

Serves 8

INGREDIENTS
30 ml/2 tbsp olive or sunflower oil
2 leeks, finely chopped
350 g/12 oz fresh spinach, chopped
12 eggs
8 spring onions, finely chopped
2 handfuls fresh parsley, finely chopped
1–2 handfuls fresh coriander, chopped
2 fresh tarragon strips, chopped,
    or 2.5 ml/½ tsp dried tarragon
handful fresh chives, snipped
1 small fresh dill sprig, chopped,
    or 1.5 ml/¼ tsp dried dill
2–4 fresh mint sprigs, chopped
40 g/1½ oz/scant ½ cup walnuts, chopped
40 g/1½ oz/scant ½ cup pine nuts
salt and freshly ground black pepper
salad, to serve

1 Heat the oil in a large, shallow pan that can be used under the grill. Add the leeks and fry them gently for about 5 minutes until just beginning to soften. Add the spinach and cook for 2–3 minutes until just wilted.

2 Beat the eggs in a bowl. Add the leek and spinach mixture, then stir in the spring onions, herbs and nuts. Season with salt and pepper. Pour the mixture into the pan and cover with a lid or foil.

3 Cook over a very gentle heat for 25 minutes or until set. Remove the lid and brown the top under a hot grill. Serve with salad.

Asparagus, Sweetcorn & Red Pepper Quiche

A rich, savoury egg custard binds together three colourful vegetables in a pastry case.

Serves 6

INGREDIENTS
225 g/8 oz asparagus, woody
    stalks removed
25 g/1 oz/2 tbsp butter or margarine
1 small onion, finely chopped
1 red pepper, seeded and
    finely chopped
115 g/4 oz drained canned sweetcorn,
    or frozen sweetcorn, thawed
2 eggs
250 ml/8 fl oz/1 cup
    single cream
50 g/2 oz/½ cup Cheddar
    cheese, grated
salt and freshly ground
    black pepper

FOR THE PASTRY
185 g/6½ oz/1½ cups plain flour
2.5 ml/½ tsp salt
115 g/4 oz/½ cup lard or
    vegetable fat
30–45 ml/2–3 tbsp iced water

1 Preheat the oven to 200°C/400°F/Gas 6. To make the pastry, sift the flour and salt into a bowl and rub in the lard or vegetable fat until the mixture resembles coarse breadcrumbs. Mix in the iced water, 15 ml/1 tbsp at a time, to form a soft dough.

2 Roll out the dough and use to line a 25 cm/10 in tart tin. Line the pastry with greaseproof paper and dried beans. Bake for 10 minutes. Remove the paper and beans and bake for 5 minutes until the pastry is set. Cool.

3 Trim the stem ends of eight asparagus spears to make them 10 cm/4 in in length. Set aside. Finely chop the asparagus trimmings and any spears that remain. Place in the bottom of the pastry case.

4 Melt the butter or margarine in a frying pan. Add the onion and red pepper and cook for about 5 minutes until softened. Stir in the sweetcorn and cook for 2 minutes more before adding to the pastry case.

5 In a bowl, beat the eggs with the cream. Stir in the cheese and season to taste. Pour into the pastry case.

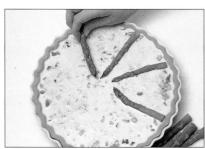

6 Arrange the reserved asparagus spears like the spokes of a wheel on top of the egg and vegetable filling, with the tips pointing towards the centre. Bake the quiche in the preheated oven for 25–30 minutes until the filling is set and golden brown. Serve warm or cold.

43

Gougère

Choux pastry, containing eggs, is very easy to make and looks impressive. Here, it encloses a lightly spiced haddock and mushroom filling.

Serves 4

INGREDIENTS
75 g/3 oz/6 tbsp cold butter, diced
200 ml/7 fl oz/scant 1 cup water
100 g/3¾ oz/scant 1 cup strong plain
    flour, sifted
1.5 ml/¼ tsp salt
3 eggs, beaten
150 g/5 oz/1¼ cups Emmenthal, mature
    Cheddar or Gruyère cheese, grated

FOR THE FILLING
250 g/9 oz undyed smoked
    haddock fillet
1 bay leaf
250 ml/8 fl oz/1 cup milk
1 small red onion, chopped
150 g/5 oz/2 cups mushrooms, sliced
40 g/1½ oz/3 tbsp butter
5 ml/1 tsp mild curry paste (optional)
25 g/1 oz/¼ cup plain flour
generous squeeze of fresh lemon juice
30 ml/2 tbsp chopped fresh parsley
salt and freshly ground black pepper

1 Place the butter and water in a saucepan and heat gently. When the butter has melted, bring the water to the boil. Immediately tip in all the flour and salt.

2 Beat until the mixture comes away from the pan sides. Remove from the heat and cool for 5 minutes.

3 Slowly work enough beaten egg into the dough to give a good dropping consistency. Add two-thirds of the cheese. Spoon the paste around the edge of a greased ovenproof dish. Set aside.

4 Preheat the oven to 180°C/350°F/ Gas 4. To make the filling, bake the haddock with the bay leaf and milk in an ovenproof dish for 15 minutes until just cooked.

5 Remove the haddock from the dish, discarding the bay leaf but reserving the hot milk for the sauce. Skin the haddock and flake the flesh.

6 In a saucepan, sauté the onion and mushrooms in the butter for about 5 minutes. Add the curry paste, if using, and the flour. Gradually stir in the reserved milk to make a smooth sauce. Add haddock, lemon juice, chopped fresh parsley and seasoning.

7 Raise the oven temperature to 200°C/400°F/Gas 6. Spoon the filling into the centre of the uncooked paste. Sprinkle with the rest of the cheese. Bake for 35–40 minutes until the gougère has risen and is golden brown. Serve at once.

Goat's Cheese Soufflé

Perfectly beaten egg whites are the secret of this soufflé, which is flavoured with tangy goat's cheese and plenty of nutmeg.

Serves 4–6

INGREDIENTS
25 g/1 oz/2 tbsp butter, plus extra, melted, for brushing
freshly grated Parmesan cheese, for sprinkling
25 g/1 oz/¼ cup plain flour
175 ml/6 fl oz/¾ cup milk
1 bay leaf
freshly grated nutmeg
40 g/1½ oz/3 tbsp herb and garlic soft cheese
150 g/5 oz/1¼ cups firm goat's cheese, diced
6 egg whites, at room temperature
1.5 ml/¼ tsp cream of tartar
salt and freshly ground black pepper

1 Preheat the oven to 190°C/375°F/ Gas 5. Generously brush a 1.5 litre/ 2½ pint/6¼ cup soufflé dish with melted butter and sprinkle with grated Parmesan cheese.

2 Melt the remaining butter in a saucepan, add the flour and cook, stirring, until slightly golden. Pour in half the milk, stirring until smooth, then add the remaining milk and the bay leaf. Season with salt, freshly ground black pepper and nutmeg.

3 Simmer gently for about 5 minutes, stirring occasionally with a balloon whisk. Remove from the heat and discard the bay leaf. Stir in the soft cheese and the diced goat's cheese.

4 In a clean bowl, beat the egg whites until frothy. Add the cream of tartar and beat until the whites form peaks that just flop over a little.

VARIATION: This recipe works equally well with strong blue cheeses, such as Roquefort or Stilton. However you flavour it, make sure you serve it immediately or it will deflate.

5 Stir a spoonful of egg whites into the cheese sauce, then pour the sauce over the remaining whites. Fold into the whites until just combined.

6 Pour the soufflé mixture into the prepared dish and bake in the oven for 25–30 minutes until puffed and golden brown. Serve at once.

Artichoke & Leek Crêpes

Versatile eggs make delicious thin pancakes to fill with a mouthwatering soufflé mixture of Jerusalem artichokes and leek for a special main course.

Serves 4

INGREDIENTS
115 g/4 oz/1 cup plain flour
1 egg
300 ml/½ pint/1¼ cups milk
oil, for brushing

FOR THE SOUFFLE FILLING
450 g/1 lb Jerusalem artichokes,
    peeled and diced
1 large leek, thinly sliced
50 g/2 oz/4 tbsp butter
30 ml/2 tbsp self-raising flour
30 ml/2 tbsp single cream
75 g/3 oz/¾ cup mature Cheddar
    cheese, grated
30 ml/2 tbsp chopped fresh parsley
freshly grated nutmeg
2 eggs, separated
salt and freshly ground
    black pepper
fresh parsley sprig, to garnish

1 Blend the flour, egg and milk and a pinch of salt to a smooth batter in a food processor or blender.

2 Using an oiled 20 cm/8 in crêpe or omelette pan, make a batch of thin pancakes. You will need about 30 ml/ 2 tbsp batter for each one. Stack the pancakes under a clean dish towel as you make them. Reserve eight for this dish and freeze the rest.

3 To make the filling, cook the artichokes and leek with the butter in a covered saucepan on a gentle heat for about 12 minutes until soft. Mash with a wooden spoon. Season well.

4 Stir in the flour and cook for 1 minute. Off the heat, beat in the cream, cheese, parsley and nutmeg to taste. Cool, then add the egg yolks.

5 Preheat the oven to 190°C/375°F/ Gas 5. Whisk the egg whites until they form soft peaks and carefully fold them into the artichoke mixture. Fold each pancake in four, hold the top open and spoon the mixture into the centre.

6 Arrange the crêpes in a greased ovenproof dish with the filling uppermost if possible. Bake for about 15 minutes until risen and golden. Garnish with a parsley sprig and serve.

COOK'S TIP: When cooking pancakes, make sure the pan is at a good, steady heat and is well oiled before you pour in the batter. It should sizzle as it hits the pan. Swirl the batter round to coat the pan, and then cook quickly.

Celeriac & Blue Cheese Roulade

An attractive dish, ideal for entertaining, in which eggs and spinach form the roulade itself while the filling combines the complementary flavours of blue cheese and celeriac.

Serves 6

INGREDIENTS
15 g/½ oz/1 tbsp butter
225 g/8 oz cooked spinach, drained
　and chopped
150 ml/¼ pint/⅔ cup
　single cream
4 large eggs, separated
15 g/½ oz freshly grated
　Parmesan cheese,
pinch of nutmeg
salt and freshly ground
　black pepper

FOR THE FILLING
225 g/8 oz celeriac
lemon juice
75 g/3 oz St Agur cheese
115 g/4 oz/½ cup fromage frais

1 Preheat the oven to 200°C/400°F/ Gas 6 and grease and line a 33 x 23 cm/ 13 x 9 in Swiss roll tin with non-stick baking parchment.

2 Melt the butter in a saucepan and add the spinach. Cook gently until all the liquid has evaporated, stirring frequently. Transfer to a bowl and stir in the cream, egg yolks, Parmesan cheese, nutmeg and seasoning.

3 Whisk the egg whites until stiff, fold them gently into the spinach mixture and then spoon into the prepared tin. Spread the mixture evenly and use a palette knife to smooth the surface.

4 Bake for 10–15 minutes until firm and lightly golden. Carefully turn out on to a sheet of greaseproof paper or non-stick baking parchment and peel away the lining. Roll up with the paper inside and leave to cool slightly.

5 To make the filling for the roulade, peel the celeriac, grate it into a bowl and sprinkle well with lemon juice. Blend the St Agur cheese and the fromage frais together and mix with the grated celeriac and a little freshly ground black pepper.

6 Unroll the roulade, spread with the filling and roll up again. Serve at once or wrap loosely and chill.

COOK'S TIP: Be sure to roll up the roulade while it is still warm and pliable, or it may break.

Floating Islands

The French name for this luscious light-as-air dessert, *oeufs à la neige*, means "snow eggs", which more accurately describes the appearance of the oval-shaped meringues.

Serves 4–6

INGREDIENTS
seeds from 1 vanilla pod
600 ml/1 pint/2½ cups milk
8 egg yolks
50 g/2 oz/¼ cup
    granulated sugar

FOR THE MERINGUES
4 large egg whites
1.5 ml/¼ tsp cream of tartar
225 g/8 oz/generous 1 cup
    caster sugar

FOR THE CARAMEL
150 g/5 oz/¾ cup
    granulated sugar

1 Put the vanilla seeds and milk in a saucepan. Bring just to the boil, then remove the pan from the heat and allow to stand.

2 In a bowl, whisk the egg yolks and sugar until thick and creamy. Whisk in the hot milk and return the mixture to the pan. Stir until it begins to thicken and coat the back of the spoon (do not allow to boil).

3 Strain the mixture into a chilled bowl. Allow to cool, stirring occasionally, then chill.

4 To make the meringues, half-fill a wide pan with water and bring just to simmering point. In a clean bowl, whisk the egg whites until frothy. Add the cream of tartar and whisk until soft peaks form. Sprinkle in the caster sugar, 30 ml/2 tbsp at a time, and whisk until stiff and glossy.

5 Using two tablespoons, form egg-shaped meringues and slide them into the water. Poach for 2–3 minutes, turning once, until just firm. Drain on kitchen paper.

6 Pour the cold custard into individual serving dishes and arrange the meringues on top.

COOK'S TIPS: It is important that the custard mixture does not boil, otherwise it may curdle. The caramel will soften if the dessert is made too long in advance.

7 To make the caramel, put the sugar in a saucepan with 45 ml/3 tbsp water. Bring to the boil over a high heat and boil, without stirring, until the mixture turns a dark caramel colour. Drizzle the caramel immediately over the meringues and custard in a zigzag pattern. Serve cold.

Crème Caramel

There are few desserts to equal a smooth and creamy, baked egg custard topped with a caramel sauce, so simple to prepare yet so satisfying to eat.

Serves 8–10

INGREDIENTS
795 ml/28 fl oz/3⅓ cups milk
120 ml/4 fl oz/½ cup
   whipping cream
225 g/8 oz/generous 1 cup sugar
1 cinnamon stick
8 extra-large eggs
5 ml/1 tsp vanilla extract

FOR THE CARAMEL
150 g/5 oz/¾ cup sugar

1 In a saucepan, combine the milk, cream, sugar and cinnamon stick. Bring the mixture to the boil, stirring, then remove from the heat, cover and leave to stand for 30 minutes.

2 To make the caramel, combine the sugar and 50 ml/2 fl oz/¼ cup water in a small, heavy saucepan over a medium heat. Bring to the boil.

3 Allow the mixture to simmer, without stirring, until it turns a deep golden brown. Dip the base of the pan in cold water to stop further cooking.

4 Quickly pour the caramel syrup into a 2 litre/3½ pint/8¾ cup mould and tilt the mould to ensure that the bottom is evenly coated. Preheat the oven to 180°C/350°F/Gas 4.

5 Reheat the milk mixture to just warm and remove the cinnamon stick. In a bowl, mix the eggs and vanilla extract. Pour in the milk mixture, stirring constantly.

6 Place the caramel-coated mould in a large baking dish and add enough hot water to come halfway up the side of the mould. Strain the egg mixture into the mould. Cover with foil.

7 Bake the dessert in the oven for 40–50 minutes until the custard is just set. Leave to cool in the water bath, then chill for at least 4 hours.

8 To turn out, run a knife around the inside of the mould. Place an inverted plate on top and flip over to release the crème caramel. Serve.

VARIATION: The custard can also be baked in a buttered mould without the caramel, as *oeufs au lait*.

Mocha Cream Pots

A luxuriously rich baked egg custard flavoured with chocolate and coffee.

Serves 8

INGREDIENTS
15 ml/1 tbsp instant
    coffee powder
475 ml/16 fl oz/2 cups milk
75 g/3 oz/⅓ cup caster sugar
225 g/8 oz plain
    chocolate, chopped
10 ml/2 tsp vanilla essence
30 ml/2 tbsp coffee
    liqueur (optional)
7 egg yolks
whipped cream and crystallized
    mimosa balls, to decorate

1 Preheat the oven to 160°C/325°F/ Gas 3. Place eight 120 ml/4 fl oz/ ½ cup ovenproof cups or ramekins in a roasting tin.

2 Put the instant coffee powder in a saucepan with the milk and caster sugar. Bring the mixture to the boil over a medium heat, stirring constantly, until the coffee powder and sugar have dissolved in the milk.

3 Remove from the heat and add the chocolate. Stir until the chocolate has melted and the sauce is smooth. Stir in the vanilla and liqueur, if using.

4 In a bowl, whisk the egg yolks to blend them lightly. Slowly whisk in the chocolate mixture, then strain into a large jug and divide equally among the cups or ramekins. Pour enough boiling water into the roasting tin to come halfway up their sides.

5 Bake for 30–35 minutes until just set. Remove the cups or ramekins from the tin and cool, then chill. Decorate with whipped cream and crystallized mimosa balls.

Crema Catalana

This delicious Spanish pudding is not as rich as a *crème brûlée*, but has a similar caramelized sugar topping.

Serves 4

INGREDIENTS
475 ml/16 fl oz/2 cups milk
pared rind of ½ lemon
1 cinnamon stick
4 eggs yolks
105 ml/7 tbsp caster sugar
25 ml/1½ tbsp cornflour
freshly grated nutmeg

2 Stir in a few tablespoons of the hot milk, then add this mixture to the remaining milk. Return to the heat and cook gently, stirring, for about 5 minutes, until thickened and smooth. Do not allow to boil.

1 Put the milk in a pan with the lemon rind and cinnamon stick. Bring to the boil, then allow to simmer for 10 minutes. Remove the lemon rind and cinnamon. Place the egg yolks and 45 ml/3 tbsp of the sugar in a bowl and whisk until pale yellow. Add the cornflour and mix well.

COOK'S TIP: The dessert should be served very soon after the topping has been caramelized. The caramel will stay hard for only about 30 minutes.

3 Pour the custard mixture into four shallow, ovenproof dishes, about 13 cm/ 5 in in diameter. Leave to cool, then chill for a few hours, overnight if possible, until firm.

4 Just before you are ready to serve, sprinkle each pudding with 15 ml/ 1 tbsp sugar and a little grated nutmeg. Preheat the grill to high.

5 Place the chilled puddings under the hot grill, on the highest shelf, and cook them until the sugar topping caramelizes by turning brown and crunchy. This will take only a few seconds. Leave the desserts to cool for a few minutes before serving.

VARIATION: An alternative way of caramelizing the topping is to heat the back of a spoon and press it down on the topping until it turns crunchy. Repeat, wiping and reheating the spoon each time.

Zabaglione

Eggs are flavoured with sweet Marsala wine to make this popular Italian classic.

Serves 4

INGREDIENTS
4 egg yolks
50 g/2 oz/¼ cup caster sugar
60 ml/4 tbsp Marsala wine
Amaretti biscuits, to serve

1 Place the egg yolks and sugar in a large, heatproof bowl and whisk with an electric whisk until the mixture is pale and thick. Gradually add the Marsala, whisking well after each addition (at this stage the mixture will be quite runny).

2 Place the bowl over a pan of gently simmering water and continue to whisk for at least 5–7 minutes, until the mixture becomes thick and mousse-like: when the beaters are lifted, they should leave a thick trail on the surface.

3 Pour into four warmed stemmed glasses and serve immediately with the Amaretti biscuits for dipping.

VARIATION: If you don't have any Marsala or Madeira you could use a medium sweet sherry or a dessert wine instead.

Right: Zabaglione; Berry Soufflé Omelette

Berry Soufflé Omelette

These are best eaten straight away.

Makes 2 (serves 4)

INGREDIENTS
4 eggs, separated
finely grated rind of 1 lemon
25 g/1 oz/2 tbsp caster sugar
drop of vanilla essence
15 ml/1 tbsp single cream
25 g/1 oz/2 tbsp butter
60 ml/4 tbsp mixed berry conserve, warmed
icing sugar, for dusting
30 ml/2 tbsp toasted flaked almonds and
    fresh mint sprigs, to decorate

1 In a bowl, beat the egg yolks, lemon rind, sugar, vanilla essence and cream until pale and slightly thickened. Set aside.

2 Whisk the egg whites until holding stiff peaks. Mix 30 ml/2 tbsp of the whisked whites into the egg yolk mixture, then fold in the remainder.

3 Melt half the butter in a frying pan and use the egg mixture to make two omelettes. Spoon half the warmed conserve over each one, fold in half and slide on to warmed plates. Sprinkle with icing sugar and almonds and decorate with mint. Cut each omelette in half and share between two people.

Blackberry Brown Sugar Meringue

An autumn variation on pavlova, using seasonal fruit and brown sugar to give the meringue a golden colour and richer taste.

Serves 6

INGREDIENTS
175 g/6 oz/¾ cup soft light
    brown sugar
3 egg whites
5 ml/1 tsp distilled malt vinegar
2.5 ml/½ tsp vanilla essence

FOR THE FILLING
350–450 g/12 oz–1 lb/3–4 cups blackberries
30 ml/2 tbsp crème de cassis
300 ml/½ pint/1¼ cups
    double cream
15 ml/1 tbsp icing sugar, sifted
small blackberry leaves,
    to decorate

1 Preheat the oven to 160°C/325°F/ Gas 3. Draw a 20 cm/8 in circle on a sheet of non-stick baking parchment, turn over and place on a baking sheet. Spread out the brown sugar on another baking sheet and dry in the oven for 8–10 minutes. Sieve to remove any lumps.

2 In a bowl, whisk the egg whites until stiff. Add half the dried brown sugar, 15 ml/1 tbsp at a time, whisking well after each addition. Add the vinegar and vanilla, then fold in the remaining brown sugar.

3 Spoon the meringue on to the circle on the paper, leaving a hollow in the centre. Bake for 45 minutes, then turn off the oven and cool in the oven with the door ajar.

4 For the filling, sprinkle the blackberries with the crème de cassis and leave for 30 minutes.

5 Peel the parchment off the meringue and place on a plate. Lightly whip the cream with the icing sugar and spoon into the centre. Top with blackberries, decorate with the leaves, and serve.

Index

Artichoke & Leek Crêpes, 48–9

Asparagus, Sweetcorn & Red Pepper Quiche, 42–3

Baked Eggs with Tarragon, 24–5

Beans: Huevos Rancheros, 14–15

Berry Soufflé Omelette, 60–1

Blackberry Brown Sugar Meringue, 62–3

Brioche with Scrambled Eggs & Morels, 10–11

Celeriac & Blue Cheese Roulade, 50–1

Champagne Truffle Breakfast, 12–13

Cheese: Celeriac & Blue Cheese Roulade, 50–1
Egg & Cheese Soup, 18
Goat's Cheese Soufflé, 46–7
Parmesan & Poached Egg Salad, 22–3

Chocolate: Mocha Cream Pots, 56–7

Colcannon, Irish, 38–9

Crema Catalana, 58–9

Crème Caramel, 54–5

Crêpes, Artichoke & Leek, 48–9

Egg & Cheese Soup, 18

Egg Flower Soup, 19

Eggs Benedict, 16–17

Eggs Flamenco, 34–5

Egg-stuffed Tomatoes, 28–9

Floating Islands, 52–3

Frittata, Tuna, 36–7

Goat's Cheese Soufflé, 46–7

Gougère, 44–5

Hard-boiled Eggs with Tuna Sauce, 20–1

Ham: Eggs Benedict, 16–17

Huevos Rancheros, 14–15

Irish Colcannon, 38–9

Lentils with

Baked Eggs, 40

Meringues: Blackberry Brown Sugar, 62–3
Floating Islands, 52–3

Mocha Cream Pots, 56–7

Omelettes: Berry Soufflé Omelette, 60–1
Omelette with Herbs, 28–9
Persian Spinach Omelette, 41

Parmesan & Poached Egg Salad, 22–3

Peppers: Eggs Flamenco, 34–5
Pepper & Potato Tortilla, 30–1

Persian Spinach Omelette, 41

Potatoes: Irish Colcannon, 38–9
Pepper & Potato Tortilla, 30–1

Quail's Egg & Vermouth Tartlets, 26–7

Quiche, Asparagus,

Sweetcorn & Red Pepper, 42–3

Salad, Parmesan & Poached Egg, 22–3

Smoked haddock: Gougère, 44–5

Soufflé, Goat's Cheese, 46–7

Soufflé Omelette, Berry, 60–1

Soups, 18–19

Tartlets, Quail's Egg & Vermouth, 26–7

Tomatoes, Egg-stuffed, 28–9

Tortilla, Pepper & Potato, 30–1

Truffle Breakfast, Champagne, 12–13

Tuna: Hard-boiled Eggs with Tuna Sauce, 20–1
Tuna Frittata, 36–7

Vegetable Stir-fry with Eggs, 32–3

Zabaglione, 60–1

First published in 1999 by Lorenz Books © Anness Publishing Limited 1999

Lorenz Books is an imprint of Anness Publishing Limited, Hermes House, 88–89 Blackfriars Road, London SE1 8HA

This edition distributed in Canada by Raincoast Books, 8680 Cambie Street, Vancouver, British Columbia, V6P 6M9

ISBN 0 7548 0323 6

A CIP catalogue record for this book is available from the British Library.

Publisher: Joanna Lorenz
Editor: Valerie Ferguson
Series Designer: Bobbie Colgate Stone
Designer: Andrew Heath
Production Controller: Joanna King

Recipes contributed by: Janet Brinkworth, Carla Capalbo, Frances Cleary, Carole Clements, Roz Denny, Michelle Derriedale-Johnson, Matthew Drennan, Sarah Edmonds, Joanna Farrow, Sarah Gates, Shirley Gill, Christine Ingram, Norma Macmillan, Laura Washburn, Steven Wheeler, Elizabeth Wolf-Cohen.

Photography: Karl Adamson, Steve Baxter, James Duncan, Michelle Garrett, John Heseltine, Amanda Heywood, Patrick McLeavey, Michael Michaels, Thomas Odulate.

1 3 5 7 9 10 8 6 4 2

Notes:
For all recipes, quantities are given in both metric and imperial measures and, where appropriate, measures are also given in standard cups and spoons. Follow one set, but not a mixture, because they are not interchangeable.

Standard spoon and cup measures are level.

1 tsp = 5 ml   1 tbsp = 15 ml

1 cup = 250 ml/8 fl oz

Australian standard tablespoons are 20 ml. Australian readers should use 3 tsp in place of 1 tbsp for measuring small quantities of gelatine, cornflour, salt, etc.

Medium eggs are used unless otherwise stated.

Printed and bound in Singapore